MINSTRELSY II

THE SONGS OF THE SOUL

DR. FORAM PATEL

Dedicated

to the hearts that feel,

to the minds that think, and

to the eyes that observe

the beauty in and of everything . . .

Contents

Contents

Foreword

"Foram Patel's poems are simple, thoughtful, and flow beautifully. They're meant to soothe as they stimulate your senses and make you reflect on the vagaries of life. My best wishes to the poet." **- Sujata Parashar** *(Award-winning Novelist, Writer and Poet)*

"Something about the title intrigued me, to think of a teacher of English as a wandering bard! and well, the poems continued to intrigue me. With simple headings for each home, the thoughts and feelings are sincere attempts to understand and express everyday issues. Whether it is the desire to be the change that you wish to see or leaving footprints on the sands of time with each small step, the thoughts are well expressed. Congrats and here's wishing you many more poems!"- **Indira Nityanandam** *(Novelist)*

*"**Minstrelsy.** Refreshing, Realistic, and True to life.A perspective on life from a woman who has risen from the ashes to be free from societal shackles and stereotypes. A woman, who has proven that old age dictates are regressive and that women can be emotionally & financially independent while looking after their homes and families. That women are human beings who can excel and succeed in every area of life - work, arts, relationships without needing to be patronized. Every poem represents all of the above and "hits the spot" in its own way."*- **Shibani Dam** *(Content Writer, Trainer, H R Professional)*

Preface

'Minstrelsy' is a production of sentiments and a chain of thoughts in the form of an anthology with 31 poems in it.

Poetry is a natural flow, a mood, and then a sitting process of drafting, revising, polishing, etc. When you're writing successfully, being "in the zone" is enjoyable and effortless, and God Knows anything can and frequently does come up from anywhere. These poems are the triggers coming from the heart and mind of a woman who has been through a lot: some observations, and psychedelic, serene, and mystical experiences. The never-ending saga of emotions: it soothes sparkles, speaks, and blasts too at times.

I'm not a writer, mostly: I'm living my simple life, managing and getting on with things as I receive them. Abrupt realignments and writing inclinations are inherently enigmatic and tend to be rude and fragmented. I don't frequently try to will myself into a state that allows me to write. The triggers—those tiny clicks that make you want to stop what you're doing and start writing—have always struck me as being utterly random.

'Chime' might be a better verb. A concept or emotion that hadn't previously been experienced in a given situation or relationship snaps into place and everything feels harmonic and somewhat realigned. I'm not making any major originality claims; as long as it resonates with me as a revelation, it's important. I also don't follow any predetermined routines or "poem traps." For me, skipping, squirming out of things that needed doing, and carving out time in an already hectic day has been a big part of creating poetry.

I believe, the more you observe, the deeper you understand and the better you write. My enjambment might have fragments of words but are tried upon the finished emotional going-through. The rhythms, typography, sound, imagery, and ideas–while you write a poem are your surroundings. Although "Minstrelsy" is a fee-flow: a flow of mood and emotions, observations and sequels.

Did I know what a monostich (one line), a couplet (two lines), a tercet or triplet (three lines), and or quatrain (four lines) mean in the writing of the poem? Not really. But it is fluid and reader-friendly when you learn them and still prefer to write your poems in free verse. When writing, it comes so easily that afterwards, I wonder why I don't always write poems. When I was very young, I found it very difficult to go through a line of the poem and catch the writer's intentions. So thought I, my first poetry should be written and composed in a way anybody can read and comprehend. If you resonate and feel through my words, the writing of these poems is successful.

Acknowledgements

I thank the spirit of an artist within me, my God within and out, a never-ending power and inspiration source. I am grateful to each individual who has crossed the path of my life and has left the footprints for me to learn something from.

Sincerely, thank you to my friends—who are just as important to me as my family and the core of my existence. They are the ones with whom I have opened up and engaged in a mutual exchange.

I am grateful for both my life's path and theirs.

I am hopeful that the readers will continue the journey with me.

Many thanks.

Love to readers.

Prologue

A collection of poems, "Minstrelsy II" is an original set of poems written in English only and stands as the second volume of the *Minstrelsy Series* by the Author and Poetess, Foram Patel. The collection's poetry was composed by the author over various periods of her life.

The notion, this or the other way, is a type of inspiration from the world, people, writing, and media the eyes and mind get to travel to, therefore the collection makes no claims to be original.

Considering the writer's limited understanding of the words' meanings, usage, and content, the emotions are tested on the verbatim.

Anticipating a substantial volume of feedback from the readers.

1. Life

In life's grand tapestry, love's the golden thread
That weaves our hearts and souls into one great deed
A gentle breeze that whispers sweet serenade
As our hearts dance and our spirits are made
Love's the spark that lights the darkest night
And guides us through life's twists and plights
With every breath, our love will grow
And in each other, we'll find our glow

Together we'll navigate life's sea
And make our love the anchor of our destiny
For love is life, and life is love
In each embrace, our hearts entwined above

2. A Woman

WOMAN

A woman, oh so fair and bright
With struggles that plague her day and night
She faces challenges with courage and might
Her spirit unbroken, her heart unlight
Her path is filled with obstacles and strife
But she perseveres, her will to thrive
She weathers every storm and test of time
And emerges stronger, her spirit divine
Her beauty shines like a beacon bright
A light that guides her through the darkest night

Her strength and resilience a sight to see
A true marvel of humanity
She stands tall, her head held high
Her spirit unbroken, her heart still flying
She is a testament to the human heart
A shining example of love and art

3. Peace of Mind!

PEACE

Peace of mind, a treasure so divine,
A state of being that's truly sublime.
It's the calm within the stormy weather,
The quietude that soothes the soul's devour.
It's the laughter of children at play,
The sunshine that brightens up the day.
It's the gentle breeze that rustles the leaves,
The stillness that soothes the restless sea.
Peace of mind, a gift from above,
A treasure that we all can love.

It's the solace that heals the heart's wounds,
The balm that soothes the soul's deepest sounds.
It's the wisdom that guides us through life,
The strength that helps us face the strife.
It's the hope that beckons us to dream,
The faith that brings us to our knees.
Peace of mind, a treasure so true,
A gift that's waiting for me and you.
So let us seek it with all our might,
And bask in its glory, day and night.

4. Friends!

FRIENDS

In the garden of life, we find a treasure rare,
A bond so strong, it's beyond compare.
Friends are the flowers that bloom in our hearts,
Their love and laughter, a work of art.
Their touch ignites a flame of joy and light,
Their words they speak, a symphony so bright.
In times of sorrow, they stand by our side,
Their friendship a shelter, a place to reside.
Their eyes see the beauty in our souls,
Their hearts understand the depth of our goals.

Together we dance, hand in hand,
Our friendship a masterpiece, a work of art in demand.
So let us cherish these friendships we hold,
Let us nurture them, let them unfold.
For in the garden of life, friends are the gold,
A treasure we keep, a love that's bold.

5. Nature Speaks!

NATURE SPEAKS!

In the forest, where the trees stand tall,

Nature speaks with a gentle call.

The wind whispers through the leaves so bright,

A chorus of creatures join the sight.

The birds sing sweet and clear as day,

Their melodies dance in the trees' sway.

The brook babbles with joyful grace,

A gentle voice that's full of place.

The trees creak and groan with age,
Their stories told in every stage.
The earthy scent of life abounds,
A symphony that never sounds.
In nature's heart, all is well,
A world of wonder, a world to tell.
The trees, the wind, the birds, the stream,
All speak in harmony, a dream.

6. The Green Field

GREEN FIELD

In fields of green, where wildflowers sway,

Peaceful moments pass, come what may.

Nature's beauty, a sight to stay,

Bringing solace, chasing all dismay.

The gentle breeze, a soothing touch,

Rustling leaves, a soft caress.

A brook's gentle gurgle, a sweet clutch,

In nature's embrace, we find reprieve.

The sun's warm rays, a comforting light,
Bringing joy, banishing the night.
In nature's beauty, we take flight,
Our spirits soaring, free and bright.
The trees, they stand, a steadfast guard,
Their leaves, a vibrant, emerald hue.
A haven for birds, a symphony,
Nature's harmony, a melody true.
In peaceful nature, we find our way,
A path to serenity, each passing day.
So let us cherish, this gift so grand,
And honor nature, with a gentle hand.

7. A Tree and A Leaf

LEAF

Amidst the forest's verdant embrace,
A towering tree, a stately grace,
Its boughs stretched wide, its roots ran deep,
A symbol of strength, a thing to keep.
Upon its limbs, a leaf did cling,
A delicate thing, a fragile thing,
Its green and gold, a wondrous sight,
A gem among the tree's sturdy might.

The wind would blow, the leaf would sway,
A gentle dance, a joyous play,
The tree's embrace, a sheltering shade,
The leaf's journey, a wondrous parade.
The sun would shine, the leaf would glow,
A beacon bright, a sight to know,
The tree's strength, a steadfast heart,
The leaf's beauty, a work of art.
The seasons passed, the years went by,
The tree and leaf, a never-dying tie,
A bond so strong, a love so true,
A story of two, a tale anew.

8. The Beauty of Nature

BEAUTY OF NATURE

In nature's embrace I find my peace,
Amidst the trees, my worries cease.
The birds sing sweetly, their melodies

A symphony that brings me to my knees.
The flowers bloom in vibrant hues,
A kaleidoscope of colors, anew.
Their delicate petals, so soft to touch,
A gentle caress, like a lover's clutch.
The sun shines bright, its warmth on my skin,
A golden glow that makes my heart spin.
The breeze whispers secrets, of the earth below,
A gentle lullaby, that calms my soul.
In nature's arms, I find my home,
A place where I am never alone.
The beauty of the world, it shines so bright,
A reflection of the love, that's always right.

9. The Beauty of Waterfall

BEAUTY OF WATERFALL

In the heart of the forest, where the trees loom tall,

A sight to behold, a wonder to enthrall,

A waterfall cascades down, a shimmering spray,

A beauty beyond compare, in every way.

Its roar is music, a symphony of sound,

That echoes through the trees, all around,

The spray creates a mist, a rainbow hue,

A sight that takes the breath, and fills the heart anew.

The waterfall's power, it flows with grace,
A testament to nature's wondrous place,
It carves a path, through rock and stone,
A glistening ribbon, all its own.
The beauty of the waterfall, it's a sight,
That fills the soul with wonder and delight,
A reminder of nature's splendor and might,
A treasure, to behold, in plain sight.

10. The Water and The Beach

BEACH

Oh, water, so calm and so blue,
Your waves gently lapping, a soothing hue,
You caress the shore with a tender touch,
Bringing joy to all who bask in your clutch.
The beach, a place of wonder and delight,
Where the sun meets the sea with a radiant light,
The sand is soft, the breeze is warm and light,

A haven for all who seek peace and delight.
The children play, their laughter and shouts,
As they chase each other, their spirits devout,
Their joy is contagious, it spreads like a cloud,
A symbol of innocence, a world so proud.
The ocean's roar, a powerful sound,
A reminder of nature's majestic all-around,
The waves crash and retreat, a constant beat,
A rhythm that soothes the soul, a symphony to greet.
The beach is a place of serenity,
Where worries fade, and happiness is free,
A place of connection, a place of peace,
Where the heart and soul find release.

11. The Sea

SEA

The sea, oh the sea, so vast and so blue
A world of wonder, a place anew
Its waves crash and roar, a symphony
A place where dreams are made, and memories be
The salty breeze whispers secrets of the deep
Where creatures lurk, and mysteries sleep
The sun sets low, the stars appear
A night of magic, a time so dear

The sea, oh the sea, so full of life

A place of adventure, a journey to thrive

Where the bravest of hearts and the boldest of souls

Can find treasures, and make their dreams whole

12. The Sand

SAND

In the hour of dawn, when night's veil departs,
The sandy shores, a canvas, bear the heart
Of nature's artistry, a symphony of hues,
A kaleidoscope of colors, as the sun brews
The golden light, a gentle caress, awakes
The grains of sand, and they, in turn, partake
In the dance of life, a joyful procession,
A celebration of the day's new fusion

The waves, a soothing melody, a lullaby,
Echoes of the sea, a gentle sigh
As the tides, they rise, and fall, and rise
In an eternal rhythm, a celestial surprise
The sand, a canvas, a work of art
A masterpiece, a treasure, a heart
A symbol of the beauty, that's within
A reflection of the love, that's been
In the sand, we find our solace, our peace
A place to dream, to hope, to release
A sanctuary, a haven, a reprieve
From the world, that's often, unkind and brief
So let us cherish, this gift of nature
This treasure, this beauty, this pure delight
For in the sand, we find our true self
A reflection of the love, that's always in sight.

13. The Sky

SKY

Oh, the sky, so vast and blue,

A canvas painted by the brushes of hue,

From the gentle rose of dawn to the fiery red of eve,

It's a masterpiece, a symphony to perceive.

The clouds, they dance, they frolic and play,

Amidst the gentle breeze, they sway and sway

Their shapes and forms, a wondrous sight

A kaleidoscope of white and gray and bright.

The sun, it shines, it beams and glows
A golden light, that illuminates the daze
Bringing warmth and joy, to all below
A celestial show, that never fades or slows.
The stars, they twinkle, they sparkle and shine
A tapestry of light, that's truly divine
A canopy of wonder, a celestial display
A nightly spectacle, that never fades away.
The sky, it's a marvel, a work of art
A constant reminder, of the beauty in our heart
A source of inspiration, a symbol of hope
A reflection of the beauty, that we can cope.

14. The Ocean

OCEAN

Oh, the ocean, so vast and so deep,

A world of wonder, a place to seek,

Its waves crash upon the shore,

A symphony of sound, evermore.

The salty breeze fills the air,

As seagulls soar, without a care,

The sun sets low, the sky ablaze,

Painting the waves with hues of haze.

The tides ebb and flow,
A never-ending show,
The ocean's might, so strong and true,
A source of life, for me and you.
In its depths, a world unseen,
Creatures lurk, both great and lean,
From the tiny plankton to the might whale,
Each one a gem, in the ocean's tale.
The ocean's heart beats strong and steady,
A pulse that keeps the world in rhythm,
A source of life, a place to find,
The ocean's beauty, a treasure to unwind.

15. The Wind

The wind, she blows so gently,
A gentle breeze, a sweet serenade,
She rustles through the trees so gracefully,
And whispers secrets to the shade.
Her caress is so soft and light,
A soothing balm for troubled sight,
She brings the scent of blooming flowers,
And whispers hope in every hour.

She dances with the leaves so free,
A wondrous sight to see,
And in her touch, we find our peace,
A solace from life's troubles and cease.
So let us bask in her embrace,
And let her soothe our weary face,
For in the wind, we find our grace,
And a love that's always in place.

16. Hopes and Habits!

HOPE

In life, we all have habits that we cling
To like a safety blanket, they're our thing
Some are good, some are bad, some are just right
But they all shape our lives, day and night
We wake up each morning with a routine
Coffee, breakfast, and then we're in the scene
We go about our day, doing what we do
But are we living or just going through?

Habits can be a comfort, a crutch, a guide
But they can also hold us back, and make us hide
From the world, from change, from growth, from life
Stuck in a rut, we're just existing, not thriving
So let's break free from our habits, let's dare
To try new things, to explore, to be aware
Of the world around us, and all it can be
And find our true purpose, wild and free
Hope, a delicate flower, so fragile and fine,
Grows in the garden of our hearts, all the time.
It blooms in the sunshine of our dreams, you see,
And nourishes our souls with its sweet decree.
But hope can wither, like a leaf in the cold,
When we succumb to habits that are old.
The weight of our routines, they can enthrall,
And crush the fragile petals of hope, so small.
Yet, with each passing day, we can break the mold,
And form new habits that uplift and unfold.
We can tend to hope, like a garden so fair,
And nurture it, so it can bloom beyond compare.
So let us cultivate hope, with care and might,
And weed out the habits that bring us to fight.
For with hope, our hearts will sing and soar,
And our souls will flourish, forevermore.

17. First Love!

FIRST LOVE

In the bloom of youth, when hearts are light,
A love so pure, it takes flight.
A first love's beauty, so divine,
A feeling so strong, it's like a shrine.
The stars align, the skies are bright,
Two souls connect, and all is right.
The world fades away, it's just the two,
Their love shines bright, like a beacon true.

Their laughter rings, their hearts entwined,
Their love so strong, it's one of a kind.
The world may doubt, but they don't mind,
For they know their love, will always find.
In the eyes of each other, they see,
A beauty so rare, a love so free.
Their hearts beat fast, their souls ignite,
Their first love, a true, pure delight.

18. Life and Love

LIFE AND LOVE

Love is the thread,

That weaves our hearts together, never to be fed

A force so strong, it can move mountains high

And make our spirits soar, like a bird in the sky

Love is the fire that burns deep within our soul

A flame that flickers bright, like a candle's glow

It warms our hearts, and makes our lives complete

A feeling so pure, it can't be beat

In the journey of life, love is the guide

A beacon of hope, that never will subside

It helps us navigate, through life's ups and downs
And brings us closer, to the ones we love
Love is the melody, that fills our hearts
A symphony of joy, that never departs
It's the rhythm of life, that keeps us strong
And helps us sing, our own special song
So let us cherish love, in all its forms
And hold it dear, like a precious gem
For it's the love we share, that makes us whole
And fills our lives, with a love that's true and real.

19. Love and Lie!

LOVE AND LIE

In love's sweet embrace, I found my heart's delight,
A gentle touch that set my soul to take flight.
With every kiss, my love for you did grow,

A flame that burned bright, and would not let go.
But then, a lie was told, a deceitful tale,
That tainted love's pure grace, and made me quail.
The sweetest fruit, now turned to bitter gall,
A poisonous seed, that would not let me stand tall.
The love we had, now tainted by a lie,
A deceitful word, that made my heart die.
I thought our love would conquer all,
But now, it's lost, and I am left to fall.
The lie that was told, a wicked deed,
A crack in love's foundation, a seed of greed.
It grew and spread, like a cancer's stain,
A poison that consumed, and caused such pain.
Now I am left, with a broken heart,
A love that's lost, and a soul that's torn apart.
The lie that was told, a wicked deed,
A deceitful word, that made my heart bleed.

20. Her and My love!

HER AND MY LOVE

My love for her, a flame that burns so bright,
A heart that beats with every passing night.
Her laughter, music to my ears, so pure,
Her smile, a light that chases all my fears.
Her eyes, like diamonds shining bright,

A reflection of the love she holds tight.
Her touch, a spark that sets my soul aflame,
With her, my heart knows no shame.
In her embrace, I find my peace,
A love so strong, it never ceases.
With every kiss, my heart takes flight,
My love for her, a love so true and right.
Her voice, a melody that fills my mind,
A symphony of love, so divine.
Her love, a gift that I hold dear,
A treasure that I'll always bring near.
In her arms, I find my home,
A place where I am never alone.
With her, my heart beats as one,
My love for her, forever begun.

21. The Beauty of Silence

BEAUTY OF SILENCE

In silence's embrace, I find my peace
A stillness that my soul can cease
From the noise of life, I'm set free
To bask in beauty's gentle glee
The world outside recedes from view
As inward I direct my hue
The silence speaks in softest tones
And all my worries are undone

The beauty of silence, a balm for me
A refuge from the world's decree
A place where I can just be me
And find solace in serenity
In silence's silence, I am whole
My heart and soul, a gentle goal
A place where love and joy reside
And peace and calm, my spirit hide
The beauty of silence, a gift from above
A treasure that I humbly love
A refuge from the world's rush and roar
A place where I can forever soar

22. Mother's love

MOTHER'S LOVE

In dreams of wonder, a mother's love doth shine,
A beacon bright, a guiding light divine.
With gentle touch and soothing grace, she doth entwine
Her child's heart, a bond that doth entwine.
Her eyes, like stars, shining bright and clear,
Reflect the love and joy that doth bring cheer.
Her smile, a ray of sunshine in the night,
Lights up the path, and doth make all right.
Her touch, a balm that doth soothe and heal,
A comfort that doth banish all fear and steal.
Her voice, a melody that doth delight,

A symphony that doth take flight.
In her embrace, a child doth find peace,
A refuge from the world's noise and cease.
For in her love, a child doth find strength,
A beauty that doth never lose its length.

23. Father's Love

FATHER'S LOVE

A father's love, so pure and true,
A bond that lasts, through all we do.
Through laughter and through tears,
His love remains, through all our years.
His gentle touch, a guiding light,
A shelter from the dark of night.
He holds our hands, and shows us the way,
Through every step, of every day.

His heart, a well of kindness deep,
A constant source, of love and hope.
He lifts us up, when we fall,
And helps us rise, to stand tall.
His love, a flame that burns so bright,
A beacon in the darkest night.
It guides us through, life's ups and downs,
And helps us find, our way to calm.
So let us cherish, this love so true,
And honor him, with all our heart and soul.
For a father's love, is a gift from above,
And one we should, forever hold.

.

24. A Helping Hand

HELPING HAND

A helping hand, a guiding light,

In times of need, a beacon bright.

A shoulder to lean on, a heart that cares,

A friend who's always there, through laughter and tears.

With a helping hand, we can face the day,

And overcome the challenges in our way.

A gentle touch, a listening ear,

Can wipe away our fears and dry our tears.

A helping hand can show us the way,

To a brighter future, a better day.
It's a gift from the heart, a token of love,
A reminder that we're never alone above.
So let us offer a helping hand,
To those who need it, near and far.
For in giving, we receive,
And our hearts are made more alive.

25. Mind of an Artist

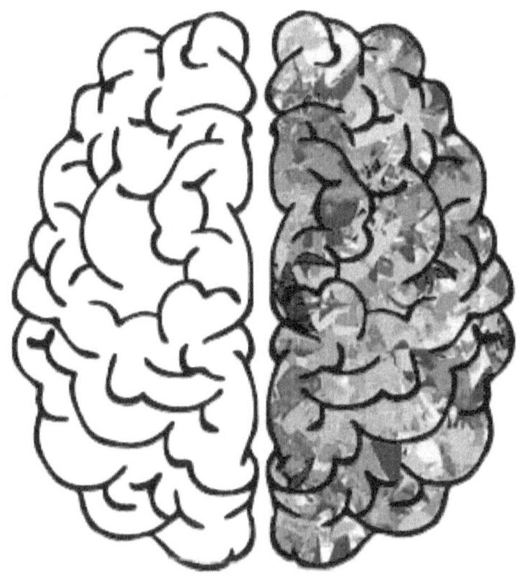

MIND OF AN ARTIST

In the mind of the artist, a world of wonder unfolds
A kaleidoscope of colors, a symphony of gold
The brush strokes dance upon the canvas, a masterful display
As the artist weaves a tapestry of emotions, day by day
The mind of the artist is a realm of pure imagination
Where ideas and dreams take shape, in every dimension
A place where the ordinary becomes extraordinary and new
Where the artist's heart and soul are forever true

The mind of the artist is a well of creativity
A fountain of inspiration, a sea of possibility
Where the waves of imagination crash and roar
And the artist's spirit soars, forever more
In the mind of the artist, the world is a canvas
A blank slate, waiting to be filled with every hue
Where the artist's vision and passion come alive
And the beauty of the world is forever renewed

26. Imagination and Reality. . .

IMAGINATION AND REALITY

In the realm of imagination, a world of wonder unfolds,

Where dreams and ideas take flight, and the impossible becomes bold.

A place where the mind can wander, free from the chains of the real,

Where the boundaries of reality are but a distant, faded feel.

In this realm, the imagination reigns supreme,

A canvas of endless possibility, a world of pure glee.

The mind can create and shape, mold and form,

A masterpiece of thoughts and emotions, forever to be norm.

But as we venture into reality, the picture begins to fade,
The colors dull, the lines blur, and the dreams are made to be
paid.
The harsh light of truth reveals the cracks and the flaws,
And the once vivid hues of imagination now but pale and
wan.
Yet, even in reality, the imagination lingers still,
A glimmer of hope, a spark of dreams, a whisper of will.
For in the depths of our minds, the imagination remains,
A refuge from the mundane, a sanctuary of sustained.
So let us cherish the imagination, and nurture it with care,
For it is the wellspring of our dreams, the foundation of our
dare.
For in the realm of imagination, anything is possible,
And reality is but the starting point for our limitless ability.

27. Life and Loss!

LIFE AND LOSS

In life, we all must choose

To hold on tight or let go

To embrace the joys and the blues

Or let them slip away like snow

We cling to what we know

And fear the unknown ahead

But loss can lead us to grow

And find a new path instead

The weight of our fears and tears

Can hold us back from soaring high
But with each loss, we gain
A strength that never dies
So let us not be afraid
To lose what we hold dear
For in the end, it's not what we have
But who we are that brings us cheer

28. Life and Lessons!

LIFE AND LESSONS

We weave our way,

Through joys and sorrows, day by day

The lessons we learn, the growth we gain

Shape us into who we are, and who we'll remain

The world outside, a reflection of our soul

A mirror to our inner self, whole

The choices we make, the path we choose

Determine the journey, and the lessons we'll use

The winds of change, they blow and sway

And test our strength, day after day
But with each gust, we find our way
And learn to bend, and not break away
The lessons of life, they come in many forms
And though they may be hard to learn
They help us grow, and make us stronger
And guide us towards a brighter day
So let us embrace, the lessons we find
And use them to shape our lives, in kind
For in the end, it's not the destination
But the journey, that makes our spirit shine.

29. Truth of Life!

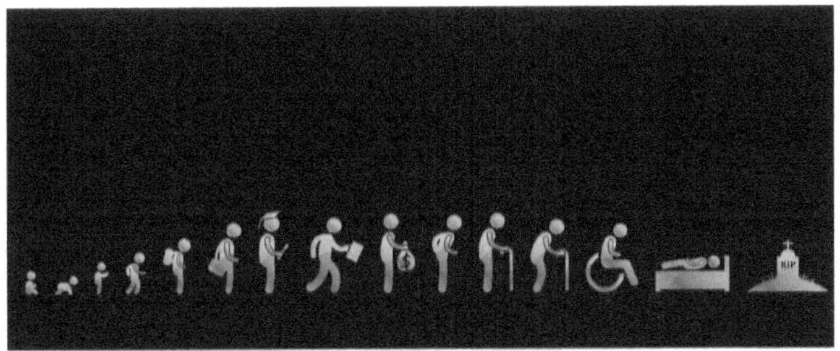

TRUTH OF LIFE

Our stories are woven in, as the fabric's led.
The truth we seek, like a gem, is hard to find,
But in the journey, we're forever intertwined.
The world outside, a canvas, vast and wide,
A masterpiece, where colors blend and collide.
The brushstrokes of life, bold and free,
A symphony of hues, for all to see.
But in the midst of beauty, shadows fall,
The truth of life, a challenge to recall.
The darkness of doubt, a veil to lift,
And in the light, our spirits to grip.
The journey's twists and turns, we must embrace,
For in the lessons learned, we find our grace.

The truth of life, a treasure to behold,
A gem, that shines, as our spirits unfold.

30. Words of Wisdom.

WISDOM

Wisdom,
A force so strong, it can move mountains high
And make our spirits soar, like a bird in the sky
Love is the fire that burns deep within our soul
A flame that flickers bright, like a candle's glow
It warms our hearts, and makes our lives complete
A feeling so pure, it can't be beat
In the journey of life, love is the guide
A beacon of hope, that never will subside
It helps us navigate, through life's ups and downs
And brings us closer, to the ones we love

Love is the melody, that fills our hearts
A symphony of joy, that never departs
It's the rhythm of life, that keeps us strong
And helps us sing, our own special song
So let us cherish love, in all its forms
And hold it dear, like a precious gem
For it's the love we share, that makes us whole
And fills our lives, with a love that's true and real.

31. Live Before You Leave!

LIVE BEFORE YOU LEAVE

Our moments bright, our memories above.
We chase our dreams and dance in the rain,
In life, we live and laugh and love,
And cherish every second, not in vain.
But life is short, and times change,
And we must leave, and move on with grace.
We bid farewell to friends and home,

And embark on journeys, all alone.
The world outside is vast and wide,
With adventures waiting to be tried.
We meet new people, and discover new lands,
And learn to adapt, with steady hands.
But though we leave, our memories stay,
And guide us on our way.
We carry love and joy, every day,
And cherish the moments, in every way.
So let us live and love, and leave,
With hearts full of joy, and souls released.
For life is precious, and fleeting fast,
And we must make the most of every moment, at last.

Writer's Message

Dear All,

Having spent years with life, as we all do, however, speculation and philosophies have different shades in the hands of writers and artists. During these years, I have learned to live in the moment wisely and be unaware of the present and the future. Predicting things takes away energy, time, and most importantly enthusiasm.

We keep waiting for good days to come which may come or may not. The beauty of life lies in its unpredictability. Imagine, we know everything about your life, we will end up mundane, tiring, boring, and tedious. Life is what we have. It is the feeling you have of being alive on this earth: we can smell, touch, see, feel, walk, and so on; and in the journey of this livingness, we create ourselves, we know ourselves, we improve ourselves, and we live - something that is possible only when you have a body and a soul together and is on this earth.

So, let's live up to the best possible way and stay ready for whatever comes.

Don't give up on life. It is one time or never.

Sending my love to my readers.

You may write your feedback to *foram.digitalaura@gmail.com*